MOST DELICIOUS QUICHE

Easy to Make Mouth-Watering Savory Pies

Amna Fadel

First Printing: 2015

ISBN-13:978-1517500771

ISBN-10:151750077X

CONTENTS

CONVERSION TABLE

- 1/2 fl oz = 3 tsp = 1 tbsp = 15 ml
- 1 fl oz = 2 tbsp = 1/8c = 30 ml
- 2 fl oz = 4 tbsp = 3/4c = 60 ml
- 4 fl oz = 8 tbsp = 1/2c = 118 ml
- 8 fl oz = 16 tbsp = 1c = 236 ml
- 16 fl oz = 1 pt = 1/2 qt = 2 c = 473 ml
- 128 fl oz = 8 pt = 4 qt = 1 gal = 3.78 L

ABBREVIATIONS

- oz = ounce
- fl oz = fluid ounce
- tsp = teaspoon
- tbsp = tablespoon
- ml = milliliter
- c = cup
- pt = pint
- qt = quart
- gal = gallon
- L = liter

INTRODUCTION TO QUICHE

What is a Quiche you ask? While it is an egg custard with flavorful filling such as cheese and bacon baked with pastry. It among the brunch dishes and is usually served at room temperature. It is also very easy to make one and you do not need to be a professional chef to make one. The filling includes a variety of ingredients like Swiss cheese, and bacon.

By now, you are already familiar with quiche. The savory and rich custard filled with things like fresh vegetables, cheese bake in a buttery crust. The quiche is the best make ahead recipe for your family lunches, dinner and even brunches. Whether you like you quiche with spinach, bacon or any other ingredient, the quiche recipes in this book will keep your family happy.

You cannot go wrong with any of the recipes here, just take your time and enjoy preparing the quiche.

21   26   28
           goat

31   32

If you want more color, flavor, and loads of asparagus pieces, it is also easy to prepare this quiche. If you want to prepare quiche in a hurry, I recommend that you prepare this.

Ingredients:

- 1 tube (8 ounces) refrigerated crescent rolls
- 2 teaspoons prepared mustard
- 1-1/2 pounds fresh asparagus, trimmed and cut into 1/2-inch pieces
- 1 medium onion, chopped
- 1/2 cup sliced fresh mushrooms
- 1/4 cup butter, cubed
- 2 eggs, lightly beaten
- 2 cups (8 ounces) shredded part-skim mozzarella cheese
- 1/4 cup minced fresh parsley
- 1/2 teaspoon salt
- 1/2 teaspoon pepper
- 1/4 teaspoon garlic powder
- 1/4 teaspoon each dried basil, oregano and rubbed sage

Directions:

1. Make 8 triangles form the crescent dough, put them on a pie plate pointing at the center of the plate. Put a little pressure on the bottom top side to form a crust. If you see any perforation, you should seal them and

spread the mustard. Set the plate aside after you are done.

2. In a large pan fly the asparagus add then add the onion followed by the mushrooms, cook until the asparagus is crisp-tender. In a bowl mix the other ingredients, add in the asparagus,

3. Place the mixture in the oven at 375 degrees for 30 minutes, to make sure the it ready insert a knife and if comes out clean then it is ready. Wait for about ten minutes before cutting and serving it.

HAM 'N' CHEESE QUICHE

I remember one time that I made this and kept it in the fridge frozen; I later came and had it for dinner. Truth be told I really enjoyed it and I think you should try it too.

Ingredients:

- 1 package (14.1 ounces) refrigerated pie pastry
- 2 cups diced fully cooked ham
- 2 cups (8 ounces) shredded sharp cheddar cheese
- 2 teaspoons dried minced onion
- 4 eggs
- 2 cups half-and-half cream
- 1/2 teaspoon salt
- 1/4 teaspoon pepper

Directions:

1. You will start by preheating the oven to 400 degrees. Spread out the pastry sheets into 9 pieces in a pie plate. Arrange the pastry shells with a heavy-duty foil. Add the pie weights followed by the beans or the rice

(uncooked). Let it bake for 20 minutes until ii turns golden brown.

2. Then remove the weights and the foil, bake it again for 5 minutes and until the bottom changes color to golden brown. Set it aside in a wire rack to cool.
3. Separate the ham, onions and cheese in the shells. In a bowl mix the eggs, salt, cream and pepper using a blender. Place the mixture into the shells; carefully cover the edges with foil.
4. Bake in the oven for 40 minutes at that point you should be able to interest the knife and it should come out clean. Set it aside to cool before cutting.
5. The frozen option; cover the quiche before freezing. Make sure that the quiche is out of the freezer 30 minutes before baking it. The oven should be preheated to 350 degrees, put the quiche in on a baking sheet.
6. Then carefully cover it sealing any loose ends with foil. Bake it and continuously check if it is ready by inserting the knife and checking whether it is clean. It should yield two quiches.

TOMATO QUICHE

My first time to see this recipe was at a friend's place and I loved it, later on, I decide that I would prepare it during a family gathering. Trust me, very time by cousin comes by he always asks for it. Very simple and easy to prepare and sure you have lots of fun preparing it.

Ingredients:

- 1 cup chopped onion
- 2 tablespoons butter

- 4 large tomatoes, peeled, seeded, chopped and drained
- 1 teaspoon salt
- 1/4 teaspoon pepper
- 1/4 teaspoon dried thyme
- 2 cups (8 ounces) Monterey Jack cheese, divided
- 1 unbaked pastry shell (10 inches)
- 4 eggs
- 1-1/2 cups half-and-half cream

Directions:

1. In a large pan, fly the onion in butter until it becomes tender. Add in the tomatoes, followed by pepper, salt and finally the thyme. Cook over the stove under medium heat, this will take about 12 minutes or until almost all the liquid is evaporated.
2. On the bottom of the pie, shells sprinkle one cup of cheese. Pour in the tomato mixture in and spread the remaining cheese on top.
3. Using a small bowl beat the eggs in followed by the cream and mix; pour the mixture into the pie shell.

4. Place the pie shell in the oven for 10 minutes at 425 degrees, and then reduce the heat after the 10 minutes are up to 325 degrees. Insert the knife in pie and if it comes out clean then it ready remove it, set it aside to cool before cutting into 6-8 pieces.

BACON VEGETABLE QUICHE

This recipe is ever changing; you can interchange the ingredients, for example instead of using the broccoli you can use the asparagus. For the vegetable you can use whatever you like, I prefer to use fresh veggies, but at times it is very difficult to choose which vegetables to use because I have many to choose form.

Ingredients:

- 1 unbaked pastry shell (9 inches)
- 1 cup sliced fresh mushrooms
- 1 cup chopped fresh broccoli
- 3/4 cup chopped sweet onion
- 2-1/2 teaspoons olive oil
- 2 cups fresh baby spinach
- 3 large eggs, lightly beaten
- 1 can (5 ounces) evaporated milk
- 1 tablespoon minced fresh rosemary or 1 teaspoon dried rosemary, crushed
- 1/4 teaspoon salt
- 1/4 teaspoon pepper
- 1 cup (4 ounces) shredded cheddar cheese
- 6 bacon strips, cooked and crumbled
- 1/2 cup crumbled tomato and basil feta cheese

Directions:

1. In a large pan, fly the mushroom, onions and broccoli in oil until they become tender. Then add in the spinach and cook until they wilt.
2. In a bowl, mix the milk, eggs, rosemary, pepper and salt. Add in the vegetables, followed by the cheddar cheese and bacon. Finish it off by sprinkling the feta cheese.
3. Cover the edges with foil. Place the mixture in the oven and bake for 35 minutes or until the knife is clear, set it aside for it to cool before cutting.

4. Freeze option: The quiche should be well covered and placed in the freezer. Before using, the quiche set it aside for 30 minutes before putting in it in the oven.
5. Preheat your oven to 375 degrees, put the quiche on a baking sheet; cover the edges with foil. Baking it until the knife once inserted comes out clean.

RAINBOW QUICHE

Filled with loads of veggies and egg cheese, it makes this quiche tasty and great for the whole family.

Ingredients:

- Pastry for single-crust pie (9 inches)
- 1-1/2 cups chopped fresh broccoli florets
- 1 small onion, finely chopped
- 1 cup sliced fresh mushrooms
- 1 each small green, sweet red and orange peppers, finely chopped
- 2 tablespoons butter
- 1 cup chopped fresh spinach
- 1 cup (4 ounces) shredded Mexican cheese blend
- 6 large eggs, lightly beaten
- 1-3/4 cups 2% milk
- 1/2 teaspoon salt

Directions:

1. Start by preheating your oven to 350 degrees. Line the deep pie dish with pastry. In a large pan, fly the onions, mushrooms, broccoli and pepper in butter until all the ingredients become tender.

2. Add in the spinach, followed by the crust, and then sprinkle the cheese. In a bowl add the eggs, milk and finally the salt and pour in the cheese.
3. Bake in the oven for 45 minutes or until when the knife comes out clean when inserted. Set it aside to cool for 10 minutes before cutting.
4. Freeze option: Carefully seal the quiche in foil and a plastic wrapper. Thaw the quiche overnight in the fridge. Set it aside for 30 minutes after removing it from the fridge.
5. The oven on the other hand should be preheated to 350 degrees, unwrap the quiche and place it in the oven at 165 degrees.

PEPPERONI SPINACH QUICHE

Some years back my wife and I had to make an appetizer for my friend's party, and this delicious and colorful quiche came in mind. Surprisingly, most of the guest loved it.

Ingredients:

- 1 tube (8 ounces) refrigerated crescent rolls
- 1 large sweet red pepper, chopped
- 1 tablespoon olive oil
- 1 garlic clove, minced
- 5 eggs, lightly beaten
- 1/2 cup shredded part-skim mozzarella cheese
- 1/2 cup frozen chopped spinach, thawed and squeezed dry
- 1/4 cup sliced pepperoni, cut into strips
- 1/4 cup half-and-half cream
- 2 tablespoons grated Parmesan cheese
- 1 tablespoon minced fresh parsley

- 1 tablespoon minced fresh basil or 1 teaspoon dried basil
- Dash pepper

Directions:

1. Cut the crescent dough into eight triangles, and put them in an ungreased pan with a removable bottom facing the center. Apply little pressure on the bottom and top sides to create crust, then seal and set it aside.
2. In a skillet, fly the red pepper in oil until it becomes tender. Add in the garlic, let it cook for one minute and remove it. In another bowl mix the remaining ingredients, add in the red pepper then pour to form a crust.
3. Bake the mixture for 30 minutes at 375 degrees or until when the knife comes out clean. Then set it aside for 5 minutes to cool before cutting.
4. Freeze option: Carefully seal and freeze the quiche in plastic and foil. Thaw the quiche overnight in the fridge before use. After removing it in the refrigerator set it aside for 30 minutes or so before starting to bake it.
5. At this point, the oven should be preheated to 350 degrees, remove the plastic and foil and place the quiche in the oven at a thermometer temperature of 165 degrees.

BACON SWISS QUICHE RECIPE

I remember this very well, it was at my aunt's place where she served us with this scrumptious quiche, it also brought along fresh fruits.

Ingredients:

- 1 sheet refrigerated pie pastry
- 1/4 cup sliced green onions
- 1 tablespoon butter
- 6 eggs
- 1-1/2 cups heavy whipping cream
- 1/4 cup unsweetened apple juice
- 1 pound sliced bacon, cooked and crumbled
- 1/8 teaspoon salt
- 1/8 teaspoon pepper
- 2 cups (8 ounces) shredded Swiss cheese

Directions:

1. You start by preheating the oven to 350 degrees. Spread pastry in a pie plate and flute the edges. Then in a skillet fly the green onions in butter until they become tender.
2. In bowl beat the eggs and add the cream, juice and mix. Then add the bacon, green onions, pepper and the salt. Pour the mixture on the pastry and cover with cheese.
3. Bake it for 45 minutes or until when you insert a knife it comes out clean. Set it aside to cool before cutting.
4. Freeze option: Carefully seal off the quiche with plastic and foil. Thaw in the fridge overnight. Wait for at least 30 minutes after you have removed it from the fridge in order to bake it.
5. Preheat your oven to 350 degrees for this. Remove the plastic and foil and reheat the quiche in the oven at the thermometer temperature of 165 degrees. You will get 6 quiches

POTATO CRUST QUICHE

All my life I have grown up in places where potatoes were in plenty and. One of the foods we cooked from potatoes was the potato crust quiche. Mama used to make this dish and everybody in the family would love it and am sure you will also.

Ingredients:

CRUST:

- 4 cups coarsely shredded uncooked potatoes (about 4 large)
- 1/2 cup chopped onion
- 1 egg, lightly beaten
- 1 cup all-purpose flour
- 1/2 teaspoon salt

FILLING:

- 1-1/2 cups (6 ounces) shredded Colby cheese, divided
- 1/2 cup chopped onion
- 1-1/2 cups cubed fully cooked ham
- 1-1/2 cups fresh broccoli florets
- 3 egg, lightly beaten
- 1 cup half-and-half cream
- 1/2 teaspoon salt
- Dash ground nutmeg
- Paprika

Directions:

1. In a bowl mix the ingredients for the crust; put it into a greased deep, pie plate. Bake it for 20 minutes at 400 degrees.

2. Remove it from the oven and reduce the heat level to 350 degrees. Then add the following one cup of cheese, ham, onions and finally the broccoli.
3. The whisk in the following eggs, nutmeg, cream and salt, pour the remaining broccoli and finish it by sprinkling paprika.
4. Bake the mixture for 40 minutes or until when the knife comes out clean when inserted. Sprinkle the left over cheese and set it aside for 5 minutes to cool before serving. You will

SPINACH SWISS QUICHE

Frozen spinach, Swiss cheese and pepper are what fill the tasty pieces of this quiche. We have this dish every year with my family. To reduce the workload you can prepare the bacon mixture one day before.

Ingredients:

- 1 refrigerated pie pastry
- 4 turkey bacon strips, diced
- 1/4 cup chopped onion
- 1/4 cup chopped sweet red pepper
- 1 package (10 ounces) frozen chopped spinach, thawed and squeezed dry
- 2 cups egg substitute
- 1/2 cup fat-free cottage cheese
- 1/4 cup shredded reduced-fat Swiss cheese
- 1/2 teaspoon dried oregano
- 1/4 teaspoon dried parsley flakes
- 1/4 teaspoon each salt, pepper and paprika
- 6 tablespoons fat-free sour cream

Directions:

1. Unroll the pastry on floured flat surface, then move it to pie plate. Then cut the pastry into two. Line the pastry with a heavy-duty foil.
2. Place the mixture in the oven for 8 minutes at 450 degrees, and then remove the foil. After this is done bake it for another 5 minutes. Set it on a wire rack and reduce the heat level to 350 degrees.
3. In a skillet, cook the onions, bacon and the pepper until they become tender, any off any liquid that forms. Add the spinach and stir and using a spoon place the mixture on the pastry.
4. In a bowl, mix the egg substitute, Swiss cheese, cottage cheese and finally the seasoning. Then add the spinach mixture.

CHEESY ZUCCHINI QUICHE

When found this recipe as I was going through some recipe books, it is easy to make and it freezes well too. You just have to thaw it in the fridge overnight and pop it into the oven the following morning.

Ingredients:

- Pastry for single-crust pie (9 inches)
- 3 tablespoons butter
- 4 cups thinly sliced zucchini (about 3 medium)
- 1 large onion, thinly sliced
- 2 large eggs
- 2 teaspoons dried parsley flakes
- 1/2 teaspoon each salt and garlic powder
- 1/2 teaspoon each dried basil and oregano
- 1/4 teaspoon pepper

- 2 cups (8 ounces) part-skim shredded mozzarella cheese
- 2 teaspoons prepared mustard

Directions:

1. The oven should be preheat to 400 degrees, on floured flat surface roll out the pastry to 1/8 inches thick circle. Then move it to pie plate, trim it the pastry. Then refrigerate
2. In a skillet heat the butter, add the zucchini followed by the onions and cook until they become tender. Drain any liquid and let it cool for a while.
3. In a bowl beat, the eggs then add the seasoning blend until well mixed. Add in the cheese and zucchini and stir. Spread evenly the mustard over the pastry shell and finally add the filling.
4. Bake in the oven at the lower rack for 40 minutes or until when a knife comes out clean. The crust should be golden brown. Cover the edge leaving a little space during the last 15 minutes in order to avoid overbrowning. Then remove it from the oven and set it aside for 10 minute before serving.
5. Pastry for single-crust pie:
6. Mix 1 ¼ cups of the all-purpose flour add ¼ teaspoon of salt, add ½ cup of butter. Then regularly add 3 to 5 cups. Add ice water and using a fork stir the dough until it hold together, and then cover it with plastic and put it in the fridge for one hour.
7. Place it in the oven for 40 minutes or until when a knife comes out clean if inserted. Set it aside to cool for 10 minutes before serving and serve along with the sour cream sour.

BACON-CHEESE QUICHE

You can have this dish at breakfast, lunch and even as dinner. It goes great with a leafy green salad; it is perfect for mix-ins. Nevertheless, you will have to bake the crust before adding any filling; this will ensure that it does not get soggy.

Ingredients:

- All-purpose flour, for rolling
- 1 homemade or store-bought single-crust pie dough
- 1 tablespoon unsalted butter
- 2 cups medium diced yellow onion (from 1 large onion)
- Coarse salt and ground pepper
- 6 large eggs
- 3/4 cup heavy cream
- 3/4 pound bacon, cooked and crumbled
- 1 cup shredded Gruyere cheese (4 ounces)

Directions:

1. Start by preheating your oven to 375 degrees. Roll the dough in a flat surface covered with flour to make 12 inches circle. Then place the dough circle in a pie plate, and then place a sheet of parchment paper to cover the dough and fill up the pie plate with either pie weights or dried beans.
2. Bake it until golden brown this will take about 20 minutes. Then remove the weights and the parchment.
3. In a skillet the butter, then add the onions, salt and pepper and let them cook for 10 minutes. In bowl mix the eggs and cream and then add the onion followed by the bacon, cheese and season with a1/2 tablespoon of salt and pepper. Stir the mixture and

then pour it into the crust and bake for 45 minutes then it will be ready, serve it when warm.

HAM AND SWISS QUICHE

A soft tender pie together with a tasty filling taste even better with a ham and cheese quiche. Everybody in your family will love it. The secret is to use easy to work with dough.

Ingredients:

- 1 large yellow onion, halved and thinly sliced
- 2 teaspoons olive oil
- 1 teaspoon fresh thyme leaves
- Coarse salt and pepper
- Gluten-free all-purpose flour, for rolling
- 1 recipe Gluten-Free Pie Dough
- 5 large eggs plus 2 large egg whites
- 1/3 cup whole milk
- 4 ounces ham steak, cut into small cubes (1 cup)
- 1/2 cup shredded Swiss (2 ounces)

Directions:

1. For this, you will need to preheat the oven to 400 degrees. Add the onion followed by the oil and thyme in a rimmed baking sheet and spread out to form a single layer. Add seasoning.
2. On a flat surface covered with flour, roll out the dough to form a 12 inch circle. Then remove it and place it in a pie plate, fold any handover and tuck in the edges. Line the pie plate with parchment and fill it with pie weights or dried beans.
3. Put the dough on the bottom rake in the oven and place the onion on the rake directly above the dough.

Let them bake for at least 15 minutes or until the onion becomes soft and the crust is golden brown. Then remove the parchment or the beans.

4. In a bowl, mix the eggs, milk, white eggs, ½ tablespoon of salt and pepper. Add the onion Swiss cheese and the ham. Then pour out the mixture into the crust and bake for 25 minutes until the center is right. You can serve while it is warm

SHALLOT-MUSHROOM QUICHE

They are many variations to this recipe, and this is just but one of them. The blistering crust makes it good for an array of fillings.

Ingredients:

- All-purpose flour, for rolling
- 1 homemade or store-bought single-crust pie dough
- 1 tablespoon unsalted butter
- 2 cups thinly sliced shallots
- Coarse salt and ground pepper
- 6 large eggs
- 3/4 cup heavy cream
- 3/4 pound mushrooms, thinly sliced and sautéed
- 1 cup grated fontina (4 ounces)

Directions:

1. Start by preheating your oven to 375 degrees. You start by rolling out the dough on a flat surface to form a 12-inch circle. Remove it and put it in a pie plate, fold any overhang dough. Cover the dough with parchment paper and fill using the beans or pie

weights. Then bake for at least 20 minutes until it brown. When done remove the parchment.

2. In a skillet melt the butter, add in the shallot and season with pepper and salt, and cook it until it turns light brown this will take about 10 minutes.

3. In a bowl mix the eggs and cream and then add the shallot, cheese, mushroom and finally season with a 1/3 spoon of salt and ¼ of pepper. Pour the mixture into the crust and bake for at least 45 minutes this is when the center of the quiche is just right. You can server when warm.

BUTTERNUT SQUASH AND BACON QUICHE

To prevent the quiche from becoming soggy, start by prebaking the tart shell using the flaky pie dough recipe. Serve it while warm.

Ingredients:

- All-purpose flour, for rolling
- 1 recipe Flaky Pie Dough or store-bought
- 8 slices bacon
- 1 medium yellow onion, halved and thinly sliced
- Coarse salt and ground pepper
- 3/4 pound butternut squash, peeled, halved, and very thinly sliced
- 8 large eggs
- 1/2 cup whole milk
- 1/2 cup heavy cream
- 6 fresh sage leaves

Directions:

1. Start by preheating your oven to 350 degrees. On a flat surface covered with to flour roll out the dough to form an 11by 15-inch rectangular shape.
2. Then move it a baking pan. Fold the edges of the dough to make the sides 1 inch high. Cover with the parchment and use the draping on the rim of the baking pan. Use the pie weights or the bean to fill,
3. Fill with pie weights or dried beans. Bake until crust is firm and edges are lightly brown in color, about 35 minutes. Remove parchment and weights; bake until bottom is dry and light golden, 10 minutes.
4. In a skillet, cook the bacon under medium until crisp, after 10 minutes flip it. Drain the bacon of any liquid with a pepper towel. Add the onion to the skillet followed by salt and pepper, then cook while stirring for 10 minutes.
5. Pour the mixture into the crust and spread it evenly. Top with the squash and add the piece of bacon.
6. In large bowl mix the eggs, cream and milk season with pepper and salt. The pour mixture on top of the filling, add sage and bake for about 45 minutes. Finally, set it aside to cool for 15 minutes.

BROCCOLI-CHEDDAR QUICHE

You can take this dish at any time, at breakfast, during lunch or at dinner. Whatever time you choose to eat it will be the right time.

Ingredients:

- All-purpose flour, for rolling
- 1 homemade or store-bought single-crust pie dough
- 1 tablespoon unsalted butter

- 2 cups medium diced yellow onion (from 1 large onion)
- Coarse salt and ground pepper
- 6 large eggs
- 3/4 cup heavy cream
- 3/4 pound broccoli florets, steamed until crisp-tender
- 1 cup grated sharp cheddar (4 ounces)

Directions:

1. You start by preheating your oven to 375 degrees. On a flat surface covered with flour, roll out the dough to make a 12-inch circle. Then place the dough in a pie plate, fold any overhang and crimp all the edges. Use the parchment paper to cover the dough and fill it with dried beans or pie weights. Then bake until the edge turn golden brown for 20 minutes. Take away the parchment.
2. In a skillet melt the butter then add the onion followed by salt, pepper, and cook for at least 10 minutes. In a bowl mix together the eggs, cream and onion followed by the cheese, broccoli florets and season with salt and pepper.
3. Mix it and then pour the mixture into the crust and bake for 45 minutes. Serve while warm

HAM-AND-POTATO BAKE

This dish it is served while hot and is crust less.

Ingredients:

- Butter, for pan
- 6 large eggs
- 1 1/2 cups heavy cream

- 2 teaspoons coarse salt
- 1/2 teaspoon ground pepper
- 2 baking potatoes (about 1 1/4 pounds), peeled
- 10 ounces sugar-baked ham, thinly sliced (less than 1/4 inch thick)
- 1 package (10 ounces) frozen broccoli, thawed and squeezed dry with paper towels
- 1/2 cup grated cheddar cheese (2 ounces)

Directions:

1. Start by preheating your oven to 350 degrees. Pour in the butter in the pan such that it covers the entire pan. Line the bottom with parchment. In a bowl, mix the cream, eggs, salt and pepper. Then drop thin slices of potatoes in the mixture.
2. Remove the potatoes form the bowl and arrange half of them in a pan. Then pour the mixture on top, press down the potatoes to ensure that they are submerged.
3. Use the foil to cover and bake for the potatoes become tender; this will take about one hour. Then remove the foil to uncover and then bake again for at least 30 minutes.
4. Set it aside to cool for 20 minutes, using a knife carefully cut the edges. Flip the pan over a plate. Then remove the parchment.

ASPARAGUS CUSTARD TART

The word rich can describe this tart. Pastry, goat meat, gruyere and cream are the ingredients that fill this quiche. You can also have it as dinner but be sure to add in green salad.

Ingredients:

- 1 sheet frozen puff pastry (from a 17.3-ounce package), thawed
- 1 tablespoon all-purpose flour, plus more for work surface
- Coarse salt
- 1 pound asparagus, trimmed, cut into 2-inch pieces, stalks and tips kept separate
- 2 teaspoons extra-virgin olive oil
- 4 large eggs, room temperature
- 1 cup heavy cream
- 1 1/2 ounces Gruyere cheese, finely shredded (1/2 cup)
- 2 ounces fresh goat cheese, crumbled into large pieces (1/2 cup)

Directions:

1. Roll out the pastry on a flat surface covered with flour to make a 14-inch square. Then cut out a 13-inch circle with a knife. Then remove it and place it on a baking a dish or pie plate. Use a folk to prick the pastry. Then place it in the fridge for 30 minutes
2. Preheat your oven to 350 degrees. Use the parchment to line the tart shell, and then fill with either dried beans or pie weights. Place in the oven for 40 minutes or until golden brown. Remove it from the oven and get rid of the beans or pie weights and the parchment.
3. Return the crust in the oven, now with the parchment and pie weights. Bake for 10 minutes until dry, set it aside to cool.
4. Boil water in a pot then add tow tablespoon of salt. Then add the asparagus stalks, cook for two minutes

until tender. Move the content to a bowl filled with ice water, when cool transfer the content again to a plate.

5. Move the stalks to a blender; add the eggs followed by the cream, flour and one tablespoon of salt. Puree until smooth.

6. Pour the mixture into the crust, sprinkle a little bit of gruyere, goat cheese on top of the asparagus tips. Bake until the crust is swollen or until it is golden brown, this should take about 40 minutes. Set it aside to cool before serving.

CARAMELIZED GARLIC TART

The garlic cloves make a delicious filling for this quiche tart.

Ingredients:

- 13 ounces puff pastry, defrosted if frozen
- 3 medium heads of garlic, cloves separated and peeled
- 1 tablespoon olive oil
- 1 teaspoon balsamic vinegar
- 3/4 tablespoon sugar
- 1 teaspoon chopped fresh rosemary
- 1 teaspoon chopped fresh thyme, plus 3 sprigs for garnish
- 3/4 teaspoon fine sea salt
- 4 1/2 ounces soft, creamy goat cheese, such as chevre
- 4 1/2 ounces hard, mature goat cheese, such as goat gouda
- 2 large eggs
- 6 1/2 tablespoons heavy cream
- 6 1/2 tablespoons crème fraiche
- Freshly ground black pepper

Directions:

1. Roll out the pastry on a flat surface to form a 16-inch circle. Transfer it round fluted pan that has a removable bottom. Cover the top of the pastry with parchment paper, and then top it with either pie weights or beans. Put it in fridge for at least 20 minutes.

2. The oven should be preheated to 350 degrees, then move the tart shell and bake it for at least 20 minutes. Get rid of the parchment and the weights; bake again for 5 minutes or until the pastry is golden brown. Set it aside to cool.

3. In small saucepan, add the garlic cloves, heat to bring to a simmer. Drain any liquid, and then add the olive oil and cook while stirring occasionally until the garlic is right, this will take about 2 minutes. Add the vinegar and water boil it and let it simmer for at least 10 minutes. Add the sugar followed by the rosemary, the chopped thyme and ¼ tablespoon of salt. Simmer over medium heat until the liquid is gone. Set it aside.

4. Chop the goat cheese and sprinkle in the tart shell, pour a spoonful of garlic cloves and syrup on top of the cheese. In a small bowl, mix the eggs, crème fraiche, cream, salt and pepper. The pour the egg mixture on top of the garlic and cheese filling, make sure that it does not cover the cheese and garlic.

5. Place the tart in the oven and bake until golden brown, this should take about 45 minutes. Remove the tart form the oven and set it aside to cool before removing the pan. Garnish with thyme and sprigs, and serve while hot.

SAUSAGE-POTATO QUICHE

You can have it at any time of the day, although you have to blind bake before adding the filling.

Ingredients:

- All-purpose flour, for rolling
- 1 homemade or store-bought single-crust pie dough
- 1 tablespoon unsalted butter
- 2 cups crumbled cooked spicy Italian sausage
- Coarse salt and ground pepper
- 6 large eggs
- 3/4 cup heavy cream
- 3/4 pound russet potato, cubed and steamed until tender
- 1 cup finely grated Parmesan (4 ounces)

Directions:

1. The oven should be preheated to 375 degrees, roll out dough on a flat surface covered with flour to make 12-inch circle. Place it on the pie plate fold any overhang. Cover the dough with parchment and fill it with either pie weights or beans. Bake for 20 minutes until golden and then remove the pie weight and the parchment.
2. In skillet melt butter, add the sausage followed by salt and pepper, cook for 10 minutes until light brown. In a bowl mix together the eggs and cream, then add the potato followed by the cheese and season with salt and pepper. Pour the mixture into the crust and bake for 45 minutes, remove it and serve while warm.

ASPARAGUS, LEEK, AND GRUYERE QUICHE

Gruyere refers to aged Swiss cheese that tastes like nuts.
Before adding, the eggs spread the vegetables evenly.

Ingredients:

- 1 tablespoon butter
- 1 leek (white and light green parts only), halved and thinly sliced, then well washed
- Coarse salt and ground pepper
- 1 bunch (1 pound) asparagus, tough ends removed, thinly sliced on the diagonal
- 4 large eggs
- 1 1/4 cups half-and-half
- Ground nutmeg
- Our Favorite Pie Crust, fitted into a 9-inch pie plate, well chilled
- 1 cup shredded Gruyere cheese (4 ounces)

Directions:

1. Start by preheating your oven to 350 degrees. In a skillet melt the butter; add the leek followed by the asparagus season with pepper and salt. Cook the mixture while stirring from time to time until the asparagus becomes crisp tender, this should take about 8 minutes.
2. In a bowl mix together the eggs, half-and-half add salt, pepper and bit of nutmeg. Place the crust on a baking sheet, sprinkle some cheese on top and add the asparagus mixture and lastly the egg mixture.
3. Bake for 60 minutes rotating the sheet, set it aside when it done to cool and serve while warm

SWISS CHARD, MUSHROOM, AND WHITE-
CHEDDAR QUICHE

This quiche combines vegetables, cheese, custard, and use a tasty flaky shell. To reduce the workloads you should prepare the pastry and vegetable the night before the cooking date.

Ingredients:

FOR THE CRUST

- 2 sticks unsalted butter, cut into small pieces and frozen until firm
- 2 2/3 cups all-purpose flour, plus more for surface
- Coarse salt
- 1 large egg, plus 1 large egg yolk
- 1/4 cup plus 3 tablespoons ice water
- Vegetable oil cooking spray

FOR THE FILLING

- 3 tablespoons unsalted butter
- 1 pound cremini mushrooms, thinly sliced
- Coarse salt and freshly ground pepper
- 2 large garlic cloves, minced
- 1 bunch Swiss chard (12 ounces), stems and ribs removed, washed and coarsely chopped (8 cups)
- 9 large eggs
- 3 1/4 cups half-and-half
- 2 1/2 cups shredded sharp white cheddar (6 1/2 ounces)

Directions:

1. Prepare the crust: mix the butter, flour and one teaspoon of salt in a blender. Then add the egg yolk and some little amount of water. Add the egg mixture

to the flour mixture and work it until the dough forms.

2. Cover the dough with a plastic wrapper, shape the dough to make a rectangular shape and put in the fridge for one hour. Cover the rim with cooking spray, place the dough into a baking sheet and fold any excess. Put in the fridge for 30 minutes.

3. The oven to 375 degrees, use parchment on the dough and leave about an inch overhang on the sides. Cover the top with pie weights or dried beans, place in the oven and bake for 40 minutes in the lower rack. Bake until it becomes golden brown, this will take about 17 minutes. Set it aside to cool.

4. You should reduce the oven temperature to 325 degrees. Prepare the filling by heating butter in a skillet, then add the mushrooms and cook until tender this will take about 8 minutes. Add pepper and salt, and then transfer the mixture to a bowl.

5. In the same skillet add the remaining butter, add the garlic and cook while stirring for a minute. Add the chard and season with salt and pepper, cover it while it cooks and stir regularly for about 5 minutes. Increase the heat to make sure that the liquid evaporates, and then adds the chard and mushroom. Set it aside to cool.

6. In a bowl mix the eggs and the half-and-half, add salt. Spread 1 ¼ cup of cheese on the tart crust, and then pour the mushroom chard mixture on top. Sprinkle the remaining cheese, and then carefully pour the custard on top of the vegetables and cheese. Place in the oven and put on the middle rack, bake for 45 minutes. Set it aside to cool then cut and serve.

CONCLUSION

Making sure that the filling does not leak through the pie chart is one of challenges that most cook find difficult to overcome. Since the crust is generally half-baked, thus you have to use a folk to prevent it from rising and consequently poring the filling.

Newer cooks came up with the idea of baking the pie shell with an extra aluminum pie dish on top, weighted with dry beans. In fact, whatever that offers weight is suitable. Beans are cheap so they make a perfect choice, but you can also use rice or dried peas. This technique stops the crust from expanding, and that your quiche will not leak under the crust. Coating egg whites on the moderately baked shell can also decrease leakage.

THANK YOU

If you have truly found value in my publication please take a minute and rate my book, I'd be eternally grateful if you left a review. As an independent author I rely on reviews for my livelihood and it gives me great pleasure to see my work is appreciated.

31837106R00024

Made in the USA
Lexington, KY
24 February 2019